ALTERNATOR
BOOKS™

T0024007

WHO ELSE IN HISTORY?

Hidden Heroes in
THE REVOLUTIONARY WAR

Elliott Smith

Lerner Publications ◆ Minneapolis

Lerner Publications Company
An imprint of Lerner Publishing Group, Inc.
241 First Avenue North
Minneapolis, MN 55401 USA

For reading levels and more information, look up this title at www.lernerbooks.com.

Main body text set in Aptifer Sans LT Pro.
Typeface provided by Linotype AG.

Editor: Brianna Kaiser

Library of Congress Cataloging-in-Publication Data

Names: Smith, Elliott, 1976– author.
Title: Hidden heroes in the Revolutionary War / Elliott Smith.
Description: Minneapolis: Lerner Publications, [2023] | Series: Who else in history? (Alternator books) | Includes bibliographical references and index. | Audience: Ages 8–12 | Audience: Grades 4–6 | Summary: "The Revolutionary War is one of the most important events in US history, but many people's stories have gone untold. Through the stories of those crucial people, readers will gain perspective on the war"—Provided by publisher.
Identifiers: LCCN 2021043294 (print) | LCCN 2021043295 (ebook) | ISBN 9781728458403 (library binding) | ISBN 9781728464053 (paperback) | ISBN 9781728462592 (ebook)
Subjects: LCSH: United States—History—Revolution, 1775-1783—Biography—Juvenile literature. | Heroes—United States—Biography—Juvenile literature.
Classification: LCC E206 .S65 2023 (print) | LCC E206 (ebook) | DDC 973.3092/2 [B]—dc23

LC record available at https://lccn.loc.gov/2021043294
LC ebook record available at https://lccn.loc.gov/2021043295

Manufactured in the United States of America
1-50869-50206-1/5/2022

TABLE OF CONTENTS

THE FIRST SHOTS

In the eighteenth century, the people who lived in Great Britain's thirteen colonies in North America were frustrated. They had grown tired of British rule and taxes.

An illustration showing British soldiers (*right*) and colonists (*left*) during the Boston Massacre

Everything changed during the Boston Massacre in Massachusetts on March 5, 1770. That day, angry colonists confronted a British soldier on the streets. The colonists yelled and threw snowballs at him. After more British soldiers were called in to handle the colonists, reports claimed that someone yelled "fire." Shots rang out, and five colonists were killed. Local sailor Crispus Attucks, a Black and Indigenous man, was the first of those colonists, making him the first casualty of the American Revolution.

Crispus Attucks

The Boston Massacre and other events led to the Revolutionary War (1775–1783). Loyalists, or Tories, were colonists who remained loyal to Great Britain. They fought alongside the redcoats, or the British soldiers. Patriots formed the Continental army and fought for American independence from Great Britain. Attucks became a martyr for the patriots and a symbol for abolitionists.

There were many heroes, soldiers, spies, and supporters during the Revolutionary War. But many of their stories slipped through the cracks when history was retold.

A RIDE OF WARNING

Paul Revere's famous horseback ride warning that the British were coming is well known in history. Two years after Revere's ride, a sixteen-year-old girl performed another important ride.

On August 18, 1775, Paul Revere rides along the streets of Massachusetts to warn people that British troops are coming.

SYBIL LUDINGTON

Sybil Ludington was the daughter of a local colonel. On April 26, 1777, her father learned that the British were going to attack Danbury, Connecticut, but he was too busy preparing for the battle to warn soldiers. Danbury was a key location because it held supplies for patriot troops.

Statue of Sybil Ludington

Sybil volunteered to make the rainy night ride on her horse. She rode as many as 40 miles, or 64 km (about three times longer than Revere's ride), waking soldiers from their sleep to join the fight. The British did capture Danbury, but Sybil's alarm helped the patriots push back the redcoats at nearby Ridgefield.

In 1961 a statue was built to honor Sybil. It stands in Carmel, New York.

SPREADING IDEAS AND INFORMATION

Information was key during the war. Many people delivered critical intelligence or spread the word about the revolution's importance.

An 1836 painting of the Battle of Yorktown by French painter Auguste Couder

PHILLIS WHEATLEY

Phillis Wheatley was kidnapped from West Africa, brought to America, and forced into slavery. She learned to read and write. Wheatley became a poet and used the power of her words to push for freedom for all people. Her *Poems on Various Subjects, Religious and Moral* became the first poetry book written by a Black woman in America.

Wheatley took a particular interest in the Revolutionary War. She saw the colonists' fight for freedom against the British as similar to the abolitionists' battle against slavery. On October 26, 1775, she sent a poem to General George Washington that she wrote for him. The poem goes by many names, one being "To His Excellency, General Washington." In it, she celebrated the fight for independence and hoped Washington would work for equality for all. However, Washington was an enslaver.

Phillis Wheatley

Wheatley was a Black woman in a nation where slavery was common, and her efforts to publish another book of poetry failed. She died in 1784 at the age of thirty-one. She did not receive recognition for her talent and patriotic inspiration until long after her death.

P O E M S

ON

VARIOUS SUBJECTS,

RELIGIOUS AND MORAL.

BY

PHILLIS WHEATLEY,

NEGRO SERVANT to Mr. JOHN WHEATLEY, of BOSTON, in NEW ENGLAND.

L O N D O N:

Printed for A. BELL, Bookseller, Aldgate; and sold by Messrs. COX and BERRY, King-Street, BOSTON.

M DCC LXXIII.

The title page of Wheatley's book of poetry

"Proceed, great chief, with virtue on thy side, /
Thy ev'ry action let the goddess guide. /
A crown, a mansion, and a throne that shine, /
With gold unfading, WASHINGTON! be thine."

—PHILLIS WHEATLEY,
"TO HIS EXCELLENCY, GENERAL WASHINGTON"

JAMES ARMISTEAD LAFAYETTE

James Armistead was born into slavery. During the war, he was put under the command of French general Marquis de Lafayette. Armistead became a spy for the patriots and infiltrated the British camp. There, he gave the British false information while providing important intelligence for the Americans.

James Armistead worked as a double agent during the war.

In 1781 Armistead learned that British general Charles Cornwallis was moving a large military unit to Yorktown, where more soldiers would also arrive. Armistead alerted Lafayette, who was able to warn Washington, who set up a blockade around the area. The Battle of Yorktown led to Cornwallis's surrender on October 17, 1781.

An engraving from 1819 showing Armistead (*left*) and others

Cornwallis's troops surrender after losing the Battle of Yorktown.

After the war, Armistead remained enslaved. He fought for his freedom and got it in 1787. Armistead added Lafayette to his name in honor of the general.

FIGHTING FOR FREEDOM

Freedom from Great Britain was at the very heart of the Revolutionary War. For some, freedom had another meaning, whether it was freedom from slavery or freedom of lands.

British general John Burgoyne talks to a group of Indigenous people. Many Indigenous people fought during the Revolutionary War.

Patriots and members of the Oneida Nation fight British soldiers during the Battle of Oriskany in 1777.

NICHOLAS CUSICK

For many Indigenous people, the war created a conflict. The patriots and the British both wanted their help in the war. Many Indigenous people supported the British, while others sided with the patriots.

Nicholas Kaghnatsto, or Cusick, was part of the Tuscarora Nation. He was a chief who decided to join the patriots. His nation had converted to Christianity and was on the side of independence. Cusick helped recruit other nations, including the Oneida.

Cusick fought in the Battle of Saratoga and was credited with saving lives as the British burned villages in upstate New York. He also served alongside Lafayette, acting at times as his translator when talking to Indigenous peoples.

Cusick's descendants would later fight in the War of 1812 and the Civil War (1861–1865).

Men fight on the USS *Chesapeake* during the War of 1812, a war some of Cusick's descendants fought in.

SALEM POOR

In 1769 twenty-two-year-old Salem Poor purchased his
freedom from slavery. He joined the Continental army in
1775 and made a name for himself at the Battle of Bunker
Hill on June 17. Poor killed
British lieutenant colonel
James Abercrombie in the
battle. Fourteen officers later
petitioned the General Court
of Massachusetts to recognize
Poor's conduct in the battle.

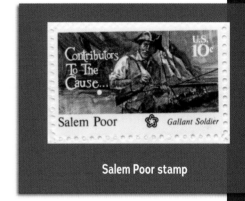

Salem Poor stamp

Poor would reenlist and fight
for America until 1780. He died
in 1802 and was buried at Copps
Hill Burial Ground near Boston. Poor's actions were noted on a
postage stamp celebrating the two hundredth anniversary of
Bunker Hill in 1975.

"We declare that a negro man,
called Salem Poor . . . in the late battle at
Charlestown, behaved like an experienced officer,
as well as an excellent soldier."

—GENERAL COURT OF MASSACHUSETTS, PETITION

COLONEL TYE

Colonel Tye, also known as Titus Cornelius, joined hundreds of enslaved men in New Jersey to fight on the British side of the war. Tye utilized his knowledge of the area to do quick-strike raids that were often against enslavers. His unit was very effective, and the British gave him the honorary title of colonel.

Tye was a key member of the Black Brigade, a group of Black loyalists, who joined with the Queen's Rangers, a British military unit. In 1780 Tye was shot in the wrist during a raid. He soon developed lockjaw and died. The Black Brigade continued.

CRITICAL THINKING

Why do you think some enslaved people fought for the British instead of the colonists or the colonists instead of the British? What side would you have taken?

From an Original Drawing in the Possession of James Boswell Esq:

Many people of color and Indigenous people fought during the war. Thayendanegea, also known as Joseph Brant, was a Mohawk chief who fought in the Revolutionary War as well as other wars.

TAKING ACTION

During the Revolutionary War, men believed women should not be allowed to be soldiers. Still, many women took action and took on several other roles to assist the cause. And many women chose to fight.

An 1845 painting by William Ranney showing the Battle of Cowpens

DEBORAH SAMPSON

Many people were passionate about ending British rule over the colonies and wanted to do whatever they could to help. For twenty-two-year-old Deborah Sampson, that meant fighting.

Illustration of Deborah Sampson from 1797

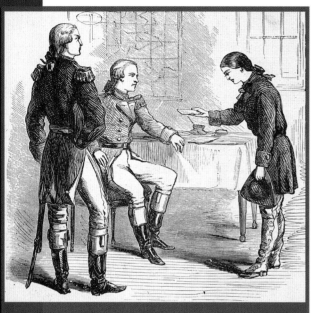

Sampson, disguised as Robert Shurtleff, brings a letter to George Washington.

Since women were not allowed to be soldiers, Sampson disguised herself as a man. As Robert Shurtleff, she signed up for war and joined the Fourth Massachusetts Regiment. She scouted, dug trenches, endured cannon fire, and led raids against British supporters.

When she was wounded, she hid her wounds so people wouldn't find out she was a woman. She had served for nearly two years when she became ill and lost consciousness. Then her secret was discovered, and she was honorably discharged, or allowed to leave the army, in 1783.

Sampson would later go on a lecture tour to discuss her war experiences. She would be the only woman to earn a full military pension in the Revolutionary War.

CATHERINE MOORE BARRY

Catherine Moore Barry was a South Carolina native. She worked alongside her husband when he signed up for the war. She acted as a scout and spy and sometimes fought next to him.

On January 17, 1781, word reached Barry that Tory soldiers were approaching the area. Barry reacted quickly. She hopped on her horse and began riding through the wilderness.

Barry warned neighbors and rallied soldiers to meet and defeat the British. Barry's actions, which included setting a trap for Cornwallis, helped the patriots win the Battle of Cowpens. The victory led to Cornwallis's retreat out of South Carolina.

Barry received several commendations for her actions. She died in 1823, but her family home remains a tourist attraction in Roebuck, South Carolina.

CRITICAL THINKING

Why is it important for people of all genders to have equal rights? How would you feel if you weren't allowed to do something based on your gender?

A HELPING HAND

During the Revolutionary War, there were many people who aided the patriots. One such person was a Spanish general.

In 1781 Bernardo de Gálvez fights during the Siege of Pensacola.

BERNARDO DE GÁLVEZ

General Bernardo de Gálvez was the governor of the territory of Louisiana. Although Spain had not declared war against Britain, de Gálvez helped Washington by blocking British ships along the Mississippi River and providing food for soldiers. In June 1779 Spain officially joined the war against Britain.

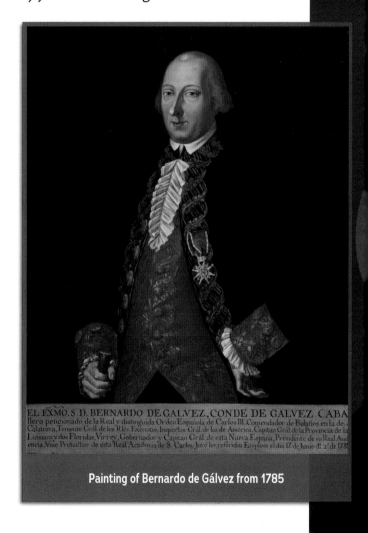

EL EXMO. S. D. BERNARDO DE GALVEZ, CONDE DE GALVEZ, CABA
llero pencionado de la Real y distinguida Orden Española de Carlos III. Comendador de Bolaños en la de
Calatrava, Teniente Grãl. de los Rls. Exercitos, Inspector Grãl. de los de América, Capitan Grãl. de la Provincia de la
Lusiana y dos Floridas, Virrey, Gobernador y Capitan Grãl. de esta Nueva España, Presidente de su Real Aud
encia, Vize Protector de esta Real Academia de S. Carlos. Juró los referidos Empleos el dia 17 de Junio d. a. de 1785.

Painting of Bernardo de Gálvez from 1785

By giving the patriots supplies, de Gálvez helped them win the Battle of Yorktown. Here, Cornwallis surrenders to Washington.

De Gálvez helped organize a group of Black, Indigenous, and Spanish soldiers to attack British forts in New Orleans, Louisiana. He also led battles in Alabama and Florida.

De Gálvez used his relationship with Cuba to help the patriots and delivered key supplies before they battled the British at Yorktown. Washington invited de Gálvez to march alongside him at the victory parade on July 4, 1783, a sign of how much the Spanish general meant to the cause.

CRITICAL THINKING
Why do you think nations like Spain and Cuba got involved in the Revolutionary War?

REMEMBERING THE HIDDEN HEROES

The Revolutionary War was an important turning point in the formation of the United States. And while many of the participants have become key historical figures, the stories of numerous heroes, patriots, and revolutionaries have gone untold—yet they made important and often history-defining contributions to the formation of the country.

James Armistead Lafayette (*right*) was an enslaved man who fought during the Revolutionary War.

TIMELINE

1770: Crispus Attucks is killed in the Boston Massacre on March 5.

1773: Phillis Wheatley's *Poems on Various Subjects, Religious and Moral* is published.

1775: Salem Poor fights at the Battle of Bunker Hill, the first major conflict of the war, in June.

Colonel Tye escapes slavery and joins the British army in November.

1777: Nicholas Cusick fights in the Battle of Saratoga.

Sybil Ludington embarks on her nighttime ride in April to warn of a British invasion.

1779: Spain declares war against Britain in June, and Bernardo de Gálvez proves to be a key ally for the patriots.

1781: Catherine Moore Barry's advance warning helps the Americans earn a key victory in January at the Battle of Cowpens in South Carolina.

James Armistead's spying on the British army helps the Americans win the Battle of Yorktown in October.

1782: Deborah Sampson joins the Fourth Massachusetts Regiment under the disguise of Robert Shurtleff.

Glossary

abolitionist: a person who fights against slavery

blockade: to stop movement going into and out of a place

casualty: a person who is hurt or killed in an event

colony: a group of people from one country who build a settlement in another territory or land

Indigenous: the first people who lived in any region

infiltrate: to enter secretly

lockjaw: an early symptom of the disease tetanus that affects the muscles

martyr: a person who suffers greatly or dies for a cause

pension: a sum paid regularly to a person who has retired from work

territory: an area of land that belongs to a country

Source Notes

10 Phillis Wheatley, *His Excellency General Washington*, Poets.org, accessed August 30, 2021, https://poets.org/poem /his-excellency-general-washington.

17 Kathy Weiser-Alexander, "Salem Poor—From Slave to Hero," Legends of America, updated February 2021, https:// www.legendsofamerica.com/salem-poor/.

Learn More

American Revolution
https://kids.britannica.com/kids/article/American
-Revolution/353711

American Revolution Timeline
https://www.battlefields.org/learn/articles/american-revolution
-timeline

American Spies of the Revolution
https://www.mountvernon.org/george-washington/the
-revolutionary-war/spying-and-espionage/american-spies-of-the
-revolution/

Harper, Judith E. *African Americans and the Revolutionary War.*
Mankato, MN: Child's World, 2021.

London, Martha. *Revolutionary War Spy Stories.* Mankato, MN: Child's
World, 2020.

Marsico, Katie. *Sybil Ludington's Revolutionary War Story.* Minneapolis:
Lerner Publications, 2018.

Revolutionary War Battle Map—American Battlefield Trust
https://www.battlefields.org/learn/battles?historical_period=72

Women—American Revolution
https://www.ducksters.com/history/american_revolution/women
_revolutionary_war.php

Index

Photo Acknowledgments

Image credits: GL Archive/Alamy Stock Photo, p. 4; Archive Photos/Getty Images, p. 5; Interim Archives/Getty Images, p. 6; Anthony22/Wikimedia Commons (CC Share-Alike 3.0), p. 7; Courtesy of PHGCOM/Wikimedia Commons, p. 8; Stock Montage/Stock Montage/Getty Images, p. 9; MPI/Getty Images, pp. 10, 19, 22; Schomburg Center for Research in Black Culture, Manuscripts, Archives and Rare Books Division, p. 11; Everett Collection Inc/Alamy Stock Photo, p. 12; Architect of the Capitol, p. 13; The Print Collector/Print Collector/Getty Images, p. 14; PHAS/Universal Images Group/Getty Images, p. 15; Bettmann/Getty Images, p. 16; Courtesy of the USPS, p. 17; South Carolina Statehouse via the Smithsonian, p. 20; Hulton Archive/Getty Images, p. 21; Wikimedia Commons (CC SA 4.0), p. 24; Museo Nacional de Historia, Ciudad de México via Wikimedia Commons, p. 25; Ed Vebell/Getty Images, p. 26; Interim Archives/Getty Images, p. 27.

Cover images: Hulton Archive/Getty Images; Stock Montage/Stock Montage/Getty Images; Archive Photos/Getty Images.